The Bear Went Over the Mountain

and Other Bear Songs

Illustrated by Maggie Swanson

Cartwheel
·B·O·O·K·S· ®
SCHOLASTIC INC.
New York Toronto London Auckland Sydney

ISBN 0-590-20306-1

Copyright © 1995 by Scholastic Inc.
Illustrations copyright © 1995 by Maggie Swanson.
All rights reserved. Published by Scholastic Inc.
CARTWHEEL BOOKS is a registered trademark of Scholastic Inc.

12 11 10 9 8 7 6 5 4 3 2 1   5 6 7 8 9/9 0/0

Printed in the U.S.A.   24

First Scholastic printing, January 1995

Contents

The Bear Went Over the Mountain

The bear went over the mountain,
The bear went over the mountain,
The bear went over the mountain,
To see what he could see.

And all that he could see,
And all that he could see
Was the other side of the mountain,
The other side of the mountain,
The other side of the mountain
Was all that he could see.

This Old Bear

(sung to the tune of This Old Man)

This old bear, he played one;
He played knickknack on my thumb.
With a knickknack, paddywhack,
Give a dog a bone;
This old bear came rolling home.

This old bear, he played two;
He played knickknack on my shoe.
With a knickknack, paddywhack,
Give a dog a bone;
This old bear came rolling home.

This old bear, he played three;
He played knickknack on my knee.
With a knickknack, paddywhack,
Give a dog a bone;
This old bear came rolling home.

This old bear, he played four;
He played knickknack on my door.
With a knickknack, paddywhack,
Give a dog a bone;
This old bear came rolling home.

This old bear, he played five;
He played knickknack on my hive.
With a knickknack, paddywhack,
Give a dog a bone;
This old bear came rolling home.

This old bear, he played six;
He played knickknack on my sticks.
With a knickknack, paddywhack,
Give a dog a bone;
This old bear came rolling home.

This old bear, he played seven;
He played knickknack up in heaven.
With a knickknack, paddywhack,
Give a dog a bone;
This old bear came rolling home.

This old bear, he played eight;
He played knickknack on my gate.
With a knickknack, paddywhack,
Give a dog a bone;
This old bear came rolling home.

This old bear, he played nine;
He played knickknack on my spine.
With a knickknack, paddywhack,
Give a dog a bone;
This old bear came rolling home.

This old bear, he played ten;
He played knickknack once again.
With a knickknack, paddywhack,
Give a dog a bone;
This old bear came rolling home.

FUZZY
WUZZY

TOYS

Fuzzy Wuzzy

Fuzzy Wuzzy was a bear.
Fuzzy Wuzzy had no hair.
Fuzzy Wuzzy wasn't fuzzy,
Was he?

Goldilocks and the Three Bears

One day the bears went walkin'
In the cool woods, stalkin'.
Along came a girl.
(A girl with blonde hair.)

Her name was Goldilocks,
And on their door she knocked.
But, no one was there.
No one was there.

She walked right in
And made herself at home,
Because she didn't care.
No, she didn't care.

She ate up their porridge,
And licked the bowl,
Because she didn't care.
No, she didn't care.

15

She strolled right over
And SAT DOWN HARD.
She broke the bear's chair.
But she didn't care.

She lay on a bed
and fell fast asleep,
Because she didn't care.
No, she didn't care.

Then... Home! Home! Home came the three bears.
"Someone's been eating my porridge," said the papa bear.
"Someone's been eating my porridge," said the mama bear.
"Hey, Mama Big Bear," said the little wee bear,
"Someone has broken my chair!"

Well, Goldilocks, she woke up,
And broke up the party,
And she beat it out of there.
And that is the story of the three bears!

Mary Had a Little Bear

(sung to the tune of Mary Had a Little Lamb)

Mary had a little bear,
Little bear, little bear.
Mary had a little bear,
Who wore a bright red bow.

Everywhere that Mary went,
Mary went, Mary went.
Everywhere that Mary went,
The bear was sure to go.

He went with her to school one day,
School one day, school one day.
He went with her to school one day,
To be her "Show and Tell."

It made the children laugh and play,
Laugh and play, laugh and play.
It made the children laugh and play,
To see him dance so well.

Why does the bear love Mary so,
Mary so, Mary so?
Because she loves him too, you know;
That's why he loves her so.

Mary had a little bear,
Little bear, little bear.
Mary had a little bear,
Who wore a bright red bow.

The Bear's Year
(with fingerplays)

Here is a cave.
Inside is a bear.
In spring he comes out,
To get some fresh air.

(Make a fist.)

(Put thumb
inside fist.)

(Pop thumb
out and wiggle it.)

He stays out all summer
In the sunshine and heat.
He hunts in the forest
For berries to eat.

(Move thumb around
in a circle.)

Late in the fall,
He hurries inside
His warm little cave,
And there he will hide.

(Put thumb back
inside fist.)

Snow covers the cave
Like a fluffy white rug.
Inside the bear sleeps
All cozy and snug —
All winter long!

(Wiggle fingers
of both hands
to look like
falling snow.)

(Cover fist with
other hand.)

We're Going on a
Bear Hunt!

We're going on a bear hunt!
We're gonna catch a big one.
We're not afraid, no way!

Uh-oh! Grass!
We can't go over it.
We can't go under it.
We've got to go through it!

Swish swish!
Swish swish!

We're going on a bear hunt!
We're gonna catch a big one.
We're not afraid, no way!

Uh-oh! A stream!
We can't go over it.
We can't go under it.
We've got to go through it!

Splash plunk!
Splash plunk!

We're going on a bear hunt!
We're gonna catch a big one.
We're not afraid, no way!

Uh-oh! A forest!
We can't go over it.
We can't go under it.
We've got to go through it!

Crackle crunch!
Crackle crunch!

We're going on a bear hunt!
We're gonna catch a big one.
We're not afraid, no way!

Uh-oh! A cave!
We can't go over it.
We can't go under it.
We've got to go through it!

Tippytoe!
Tippytoe!

Shhh! Do you see what I see?
Two furry brown ears!
Two huge staring eyes!
Oh, no! It's a bear!

RUN!

Back through the cave! Tippytoe! Tippytoe!
Back through the forest! Crackle crunch! Crackle crunch!
Back through the stream! Splash plunk! Splash plunk!
Back through the grass! Swish swish! Swish swish!

Back to our house!
Dash upstairs!
Run into the bedroom!
Dive into bed!
Hide under the covers!

Whew! We're not going on a
bear hunt again!